THE BEGINNER'S GUIDE TO INVESTMENT

How to Invest Rightly

Victor Enite Ofolu

ISBN-13: 9798854182379
ISBN-10: 1477123456

Cover design by: Art Painter
Library of Congress Control Number: 2018675309
Printed in the United States of America

I dedicate this book to the Almighty God who gave me inspiration, wisdom, and knowledge, and also to my dear parents (Mr. and Mrs. J.J. Ofolu)

CONTENTS

INTRODUCTION

Welcome to the "Beginner's Guide to Investment: How to Invest Rightly" This guide simplifies investing complexities, exploring concepts, asset classes, and strategies. Learn about stocks, bonds, real estate, and more, building a balanced investment plan aligned with your goals. Uncover key principles like diversification and risk management for confidence in the investment landscape. Start your journey to financial growth and prosperity today! Empower yourself with the knowledge and confidence to make informed investment decisions, whether you're saving, building wealth, or securing your future. Let's embark on this exciting expedition into the world of investing!

CHAPTER1: UNDERSTANDING INVESTMENT

1.1 What is Investment?

Investment refers to the process of allocating money or resources with the expectation of generating profits or returns over time. Instead of keeping your money idle, investing allows you to potentially grow your wealth by putting it to work in various financial assets or ventures.

1.2 Why Invest?

Investing offers several benefits:

Potential for Growth: By investing, you can aim to earn higher returns than what traditional savings accounts offer, enabling your wealth to grow over time.

Beat Inflation: Investing helps you outpace the effects of inflation, ensuring that your money retains its purchasing power.

Achieve Financial Goals: Whether it's saving for retirement, buying a home, or funding your child's education, investment can help you reach your long-term financial goals.

1.3 Key Investment Terms Simplified

To navigate the investment world, it's important to understand some common terms:

Asset: Anything with monetary value that can be bought or sold, such as stocks, bonds, real estate, or commodities.

Portfolio: The collection of investments you hold, including stocks, bonds, and other assets.

Return: The gain or loss you make on an investment, usually expressed as a percentage.

Risk: The possibility of losing some or all of your investment due to market fluctuations or other factors.

Diversification: Spreading your investments across different asset classes and industries to reduce risk.

Liquidity: The ease with which an investment can be converted into cash without impacting its market price.

Understanding these terms will help you communicate effectively and make informed investment decisions.

In the next chapter, we'll explore the importance of setting financial goals and how they influence your investment strategy

CHAPTER 2: SETTING FINANCIAL GOALS

2.1 The Importance of Financial Goals

Before diving into the world of investing, it's crucial to establish clear financial goals. Financial goals provide direction and purpose to your investment strategy. They help you prioritize your objectives, make informed decisions, and stay focused on what matters most to you. Setting specific financial goals allows you to measure your progress and make adjustments along the way.

2.2 Identifying Short-term and Long-term Goals

Financial goals can be categorized into short-term and long-term objectives. Short-term goals typically span a period of one to three years and may include building an emergency fund, saving for a vacation, or purchasing a new car. Long-term goals, on the other hand, have a time horizon of five years or more and often involve bigger aspirations such as buying a house, funding your children's education, or planning for retirement.

When identifying your goals, consider the timeframe, the amount of money required, and the level of priority for each objective. This will help you allocate your resources and investments accordingly.

2.3 SMART Goal Setting

To set effective financial goals, follow the **SMART** framework:

Specific: Clearly define your goals. For example, instead of saying "I want to save money," specify the amount and purpose like "I want to save $10,000 for a down payment on a house."

Measurable: Make your goals quantifiable so that you can track your progress. Assign specific numbers, percentages, or deadlines to your goals.

Achievable: Ensure that your goals are realistic and attainable. Consider your income, expenses, and other financial obligations when setting targets.

Relevant: Align your goals with your values and aspirations. Choose objectives that are meaningful and significant to you personally.

Time-Bound: Set a timeframe or deadline for achieving your goals. This creates a sense of urgency and helps you stay on track. By following the SMART approach, you can establish well-defined financial goals that provide a roadmap for your investment journey.

In the next chapter, we'll explore the importance of building a strong financial foundation before diving into investment opportunities.

CHAPTER 3: BUILDING A STRONG FINANCIAL FOUNDATION

3.1 Creating an Emergency Fund

An emergency fund is a crucial component of a strong financial foundation. It's a pool of money set aside to cover unexpected expenses or financial emergencies. Aim to save three to six months' worth of living expenses in an easily accessible and low-risk account. This fund acts as a safety net, providing peace of mind and protecting you from going into debt during challenging times.

3.2 Clearing Debt and Managing Expenses

To build a solid financial foundation, it's important to address any outstanding debt. Start by listing all your debts, such as credit card balances, student loans, or outstanding loans. Develop a repayment plan by prioritizing high-interest debts and making consistent payments to reduce your overall debt burden.

Managing expenses is equally important. Create a budget that tracks your income and expenses. Identify areas where you can reduce unnecessary spending and allocate more money towards debt repayment and saving. By living within your means and controlling expenses, you'll have more resources available for investing.

3.3 Budgeting Basics

Budgeting involves tracking your income and expenses to ensure that you're allocating your money effectively. Here are some budgeting basics to consider:

List all your sources of income, including your salary, freelance work, or any other income streams.
Categorize your expenses into fixed (e.g., rent, utilities) and variable (e.g., entertainment, dining out).
Determine how much you can allocate to different expense categories and savings.
Track your spending regularly and review your budget to make adjustments as needed.
Budgeting helps you gain a clear understanding of your financial situation and supports your efforts to save and invest more effectively.

Building a strong financial foundation through emergency funds, debt management, and budgeting sets you up for success when it comes to investing. In the next chapter, we'll explore different types of investments and their characteristics.

CHAPTER 4: TYPES OF INVESTMENTS

4.1 Stocks

Stocks represent ownership shares in a company. When you buy stocks, you become a shareholder and have the potential to benefit from the company's profits and growth. Stock prices can fluctuate based on various factors such as company performance, market conditions, and investor sentiment.

4.2 Bonds

Bonds are debt instruments issued by governments, municipalities, or corporations. When you buy a bond, you're essentially lending money to the issuer in exchange for regular interest payments and the return of the principal amount at maturity. Bonds are generally considered lower risk compared to stocks but offer lower potential returns.

4.3 Mutual Funds

Mutual funds pool money from multiple investors to invest in a diversified portfolio of stocks, bonds, or other assets. They are managed by professional fund managers who make investment decisions on behalf of the investors. Mutual funds offer diversification and are suitable for those seeking a hands-off approach to investing.

4.4 Exchange-Traded Funds (ETFs)

ETFs are similar to mutual funds but are traded on stock exchanges like individual stocks. They offer diversification and allow investors to buy and sell shares throughout the trading day. ETFs can track various market indexes or specific sectors, providing exposure to a wide range of assets.

4.5 Real Estate
Real estate investments involve buying properties such as residential homes, commercial buildings, or land. Real estate can generate income through rental payments or increase in property value over time. Investing in real estate offers the potential for long-term growth and income generation.

4.6 Diversification
Diversification is a strategy that involves spreading your investments across different asset classes (e.g., stocks, bonds, real estate) and sectors to reduce risk. By diversifying, you lower the impact of any single investment on your overall portfolio, potentially mitigating losses if one investment performs poorly.

CHAPTER 5: RISK AND RETURN

5.1 Understanding Risk

Risk refers to the uncertainty or potential for loss in an investment. Different investments carry different levels of risk. Generally, higher-risk investments have the potential for higher returns but also higher volatility and potential losses. Lower-risk investments may offer stability but typically provide lower returns.

5.2 Evaluating Return Potential

Return refers to the gain or profit generated from an investment. It can be in the form of capital appreciation (increase in value) or income (e.g., dividends, interest payments). Understanding the return potential of an investment helps you assess its suitability and align it with your financial goals.

5.3 Risk-Return Tradeoff

The risk-return tradeoff is the principle that higher potential returns come with higher levels of risk. It means that to pursue higher returns, you may need to accept a higher degree of risk. It's essential to find a balance that aligns with your risk tolerance, investment goals, and timeframe.

By understanding different investment types, their characteristics, and the risk-return tradeoff, you can make more informed investment decisions. In the next chapter, we'll explore different investment strategies to consider.

CHAPTER 6: INVESTMENT STRATEGIES

6.1 Passive vs. Active Investing

Passive investing involves building a diversified portfolio and holding it for the long term, typically through index funds or ETFs. The goal is to match the performance of a specific market index rather than actively trying to outperform it. This strategy is based on the belief that markets are efficient and it's difficult to consistently beat them.

Active investing, on the other hand, involves making specific investment decisions to outperform the market. Active investors conduct research, analyze market trends, and actively buy and sell investments to try to achieve higher returns. This strategy requires more time, effort, and expertise.

6.2 Dollar-Cost Averaging

Dollar-cost averaging is an investment strategy where you invest a fixed amount of money at regular intervals, regardless of the market's ups and downs. By consistently investing over time, you buy more shares when prices are low and fewer shares when prices are high. This approach helps to mitigate the impact of market volatility and can potentially lead to long-term gains.

6.3 Value Investing

Value investing involves identifying undervalued stocks or assets and investing in them with the belief that their value will increase over time. Value investors look for opportunities where the market has overlooked or undervalued the true worth of a company or asset. This strategy requires careful analysis and patience.

6.4 Growth Investing

Growth investing focuses on investing in companies that have the potential for above-average growth in earnings and stock prices. Growth investors seek out companies in rapidly expanding industries or with innovative products or services. This strategy prioritizes capital appreciation over dividend payments.

6.5 Dividend Investing

Dividend investing involves investing in companies that consistently pay dividends to their shareholders. Dividend investors prioritize regular income generation rather than solely relying on capital appreciation. This strategy is suitable for investors seeking steady cash flow and income stability.

CHAPTER 7: INVESTMENT ACCOUNTS AND PLATFORMS

7.1 Individual Retirement Accounts (IRAs)

IRAs are tax-advantaged retirement accounts that allow individuals to save for retirement. Traditional IRAs offer tax-deferred contributions, meaning you'll pay taxes when you withdraw the funds in retirement. Roth IRAs, on the other hand, offer tax-free withdrawals in retirement, but contributions are made with after-tax money.

7.2 401(k) Plans

A 401(k) plan is an employer-sponsored retirement savings plan. Employees contribute a portion of their salary, often with employer matching contributions. Contributions to a 401(k) plan are typically tax-deferred, meaning they reduce your taxable income, and taxes are paid upon withdrawal in retirement.

7.3 Brokerage Accounts

Brokerage accounts are investment accounts offered by brokerage firms that allow you to buy and sell a variety of investments, including stocks, bonds, mutual funds, and ETFs. They provide flexibility and control over your investment choices but do not offer the same tax advantages as retirement accounts.

7.4 Robo-Advisors

Robo-advisors are automated investment platforms that use

algorithms to provide investment recommendations and manage your portfolio. They offer a simplified and low-cost approach to investing, suitable for those who prefer a hands-off approach. Robo-advisors typically create and manage a diversified portfolio based on your risk tolerance and goals.

Understanding different investment strategies and types of investment accounts and platforms can help you choose the approach that aligns with your goals and preferences. In the next chapter, we'll delve into the importance of conducting investment research and how to evaluate investment opportunities.

CHAPTER 8: CONDUCTING INVESTMENT RESEARCH

8.1 Importance of Research

Conducting thorough research is crucial before making any investment decisions. Research helps you understand the potential risks and rewards associated with an investment opportunity, assess the financial health of companies or assets, and make informed choices aligned with your goals.

8.2 Reliable Sources of Information

When conducting investment research, it's important to rely on reputable and reliable sources of information. These can include financial news websites, annual reports, company filings, analyst reports, and economic indicators. By gathering information from credible sources, you can make more informed investment decisions.

8.3 Fundamental Analysis

Fundamental analysis involves assessing the financial health and intrinsic value of a company or asset. It involves examining factors such as earnings, revenue, profitability, management, competitive advantages, and industry trends. Fundamental analysis helps determine whether an investment is undervalued or overvalued.

8.4 Technical Analysis

Technical analysis focuses on analyzing historical price and volume data to predict future price movements. It involves studying charts, patterns, and indicators to identify trends and make investment decisions based on price patterns and market behavior. Technical analysis is commonly used by short-term traders.

8.5 Evaluating Risk Factors

When researching investment opportunities, it's important to assess the potential risks involved. These can include market volatility, economic conditions, industry-specific risks, regulatory changes, and company-specific risks. Understanding and evaluating risk factors help you make informed decisions and manage your risk exposure.

CHAPTER 9: EVALUATING INVESTMENT OPPORTUNITIES

9.1 Assessing Potential Returns

When evaluating investment opportunities, it's crucial to assess the potential returns. This involves analyzing historical performance, projected earnings, and future growth prospects. Consider factors such as dividend yield, capital appreciation potential, and total return potential to gauge the attractiveness of an investment.

9.2 Considering Time Horizon

Your time horizon, or the length of time you plan to hold an investment, is an important consideration. Short-term investments may prioritize quick gains, while long-term investments can capitalize on compounding growth and ride out market fluctuations. Align your investment choices with your time horizon and financial goals.

9.3 Analyzing Costs and Fees

Investment costs and fees can significantly impact your overall returns. Evaluate expense ratios, brokerage fees, commissions, and other charges associated with the investment. Lowering costs can enhance your investment returns over time, so be mindful of the fees involved.

9.4 Seeking Professional Advice

If you're unsure or lack expertise in a particular investment area, consider seeking professional advice from financial advisors or investment professionals. They can provide guidance tailored to your specific circumstances, risk tolerance, and financial goals.

By conducting thorough research, evaluating potential returns, considering time horizons, analyzing costs and fees, and seeking professional advice when needed, you can make more informed investment decisions. In the next chapter, we'll explore the importance of monitoring and reviewing your investments regularly.

CHAPTER 10: MONITORING AND REVIEWING YOUR INVESTMENTS

10.1 Importance of Regular Monitoring

Monitoring your investments is crucial to ensure they are performing as expected and to make any necessary adjustments. Regular monitoring allows you to stay informed about market conditions, track the performance of your investments, and identify any changes or opportunities that may require action.

10.2 Tracking Performance

Track the performance of your investments by regularly reviewing statements, account balances, and investment returns. Compare the performance against relevant benchmarks or your investment goals to assess whether your investments are meeting expectations.

10.3 Rebalancing Your Portfolio

Over time, the allocation of your investments may deviate from your original plan due to market fluctuations. Rebalancing involves adjusting your portfolio by buying or selling assets to bring it back to your desired asset allocation. Regular rebalancing helps maintain a diversified and risk-appropriate portfolio.

10.4 Staying Informed

Stay informed about market trends, economic news, and changes in the industries or sectors in which you have investments. Keeping up-to-date with relevant information helps you make informed decisions and take advantage of potential opportunities or mitigate risks.

CHAPTER 11: RISK MANAGEMENT AND EMOTIONAL DISCIPLINE

11.1 Understanding Risk Management
Risk management involves identifying, assessing, and mitigating risks associated with your investments. Diversification, asset allocation, and setting appropriate risk tolerance are key components of effective risk management. By managing risk, you can protect your investments from significant losses.

11.2 Setting Risk Tolerance
Risk tolerance refers to your ability and willingness to accept market volatility and potential losses. It's important to assess your risk tolerance and align your investments accordingly. Conservative investors may prefer lower-risk investments, while aggressive investors may be comfortable with higher-risk investments.

11.3 Emotional Discipline

Emotional discipline is crucial in investment management. Emotions such as fear and greed can lead to impulsive and irrational investment decisions. Maintain discipline by sticking to your investment plan, avoiding reactionary moves based on short-term market fluctuations, and focusing on long-term goals.

11.4 Long-Term Perspective

Investing should be approached with a long-term perspective. Market fluctuations are normal, and short-term volatility should not derail your long-term investment strategy. Stay focused on your financial goals and avoid making hasty decisions based on short-term market movements.

CHAPTER 12: TAX CONSIDERATIONS

12.1 Tax-Efficient Investing

Tax-efficient investing aims to minimize the impact of taxes on your investment returns. Strategies such as investing in tax-advantaged accounts like IRAs or 401(k)s, utilizing tax-efficient funds, and implementing tax-loss harvesting can help optimize your after-tax returns.

12.2 Capital Gains and Losses

Capital gains and losses occur when you sell an investment for more or less than its purchase price. Understanding how capital gains taxes are calculated and considering the timing of selling investments can help manage your tax liability.

12.3 Tax-Deferred vs. Taxable Accounts

Different types of investment accounts have varying tax implications. Tax-deferred accounts like IRAs allow you to postpone paying taxes on contributions and earnings until retirement, while taxable accounts require you to pay taxes on investment gains in the year they occur. Consider the tax advantages and limitations of each account type when making investment decisions.

12.4 Seeking Professional Advice

Tax laws and regulations can be complex, and seeking professional advice from a tax advisor or accountant is advisable. They can help you navigate the tax implications of your investments, maximize tax benefits, and ensure compliance with tax laws.

Understanding risk management, maintaining emotional discipline, considering tax implications, and seeking professional advice when needed are important aspects of successful investing. Regularly monitoring and reviewing your investments will help you stay on track towards your financial goals.

CONCLUSION

Congratulations! You have completed "The Beginner's Guide to Investment: How to Invest Rightly." Armed with the knowledge and insights provided in this ebook, you are ready to embark on your investment journey with confidence. Remember, investing is a long-term commitment, so continue learning, adapt to changing market conditions, and stay focused on your financial goals. Wishing you success in your investment endeavors!

www.ingramcontent.com/pod-product-compliance
Lightning Source LLC
Chambersburg PA
CBHW072227290526
45794CB00007B/2917